WHY DO WE BEHAVE LIKE THAT?

THINK LIKE A SCIENTIST

by Dru Hunter

CREATIVE EDUCATION • CREATIVE PAPERBACKS

Published by **Creative Education** and **Creative Paperbacks**
P.O. Box 227, Mankato, Minnesota 56002
Creative Education and Creative Paperbacks are imprints of The Creative Company
www.thecreativecompany.us

Design and production by **Christine Vanderbeek**
Art direction by **Rita Marshall**
Printed in Malaysia

Photographs by Alamy (Juliet Ferguson, Bjanka Kadic, North Wind Picture
Archives, Pictorial Press Ltd, World History Archive), Corbis (AB STILL LTD/Science
Photo Library, Bettmann, Christie's Images, Tim Graham, GraphicaArtis, Colin
McPherson, Charles O'Rear, STRINGER/ BRAZIL/Reuters, Keren Su, RICK WILKING/
Reuters), Getty Images (Getty Images, Justin Sullivan), iStockphoto (ewg3D,
imgendesign, Tanuki Photography), Shutterstock (Rachelle Burnside, Sergey Chayko,
CLM, Fotokostic, hxdbzxy, Jennifer Stone, Marina Sun, Konstantin Sutyagin, Rob van
Esch, Aleks vF), SuperStock (Travel Pix Collection/Jon Arnold Images, U.S. Navy
Public Domain/U.S. Navy Public Domain)

Library of Congress Cataloging-in-Publication Data
Hunter, Dru.
Why do we behave like that? / Dru Hunter.
p. cm. — (Think like a scientist)
Includes bibliographical references and index.
Summary: A narration of the origins, advancements, and future of the social sciences,
including anthropology and psychology, and the ways in which scientists utilize the
scientific method to explore questions.

ISBN 978-1-60818-597-9 (hardcover)
ISBN 978-1-62832-202-6 (pbk)
1. Social sciences—Juvenile literature. 2. Social sciences—History—Juvenile literature.
3. Social scientists—Juvenile literature. I. Title. ·

H95.H86 2015
301—dc23   2014033142

CCSS: RI.5.1, 2, 3, 8; RI.6.1, 3, 7; RST.6-8.1, 2, 5, 6, 8

First Edition HC 9 8 7 6 5 4 3 2 1
First Edition PBK 9 8 7 6 5 4 3 2 1

ON THE COVER Apple Inc.'s iPod, an indicator of social behavior

WHY DO WE BEHAVE LIKE THAT?

TABLE OF CONTENTS

SCIENTIST IN THE SPOTLIGHT

INTRODUCTION

n 1922, deep in Egypt's Valley of the Kings, archaeologist Howard Carter broke through a sealed door and saw a stone-filled passage. Removing the stones revealed another door. As he made a small hole in that door, Carter's hands trembled in anticipation of what could be behind it.

After testing for dangerous gases, Carter widened the hole and inserted a candle. The flame flickered as hot air escaped, and Carter peered into a room. He saw shiny golden objects inside. Among the treasures were strange animal statues, boat models, and chariots. There were also two mummified fetuses and the stone coffin of a king, its mummy adorned in a golden mask. After years of searching, Carter had found King Tut's tomb!

Social science answers questions civilizations have about their ancestors and why modern people might behave the way they do. It includes fields such as anthropology (and its subset of archaeology), economics, political science, sociology, and psychology. Humanities subjects, such as history and communications, often play a role in the social sciences, too. To understand a society and the relationships of its peoples, social scientists ask questions, observe, investigate, and analyze. They test theories by experimenting. Whether it is the discovery of an ancient civilization's tomb or other intrigues—such as why people of some **cultures** shake hands in greeting, how the Super Bowl affects local businesses, or what serial killers have in common—explaining all these human behaviors is the work of social scientists.

SOCIAL ROOTS

TO UNDERSTAND INDIVIDUALS AND THEIR RELATIONships within a society, social scientists use the **scientific method** to gather information and examine what is found, just as natural scientists (such as biologists and physicists) do. Social scientists ask questions and try to answer them with proof.

Since ancient times, people have been fascinated with the brain and how it affects behavior. A Greek doctor named Galen, who lived in the second century A.D., used his work on wounded gladiators and dissections of animals to **hypothesize** how the brain functioned. From his experiments on ox, pig, and primate brains, he was able to show that the control center was in the head, not the heart, as earlier thinkers had believed. Galen's book *On the Diagnosis and Cure of the Soul's Passion* discussed how to cure mental problems by having the afflicted person talk to an older male about their secrets and desires. Galen's brain theories influenced scientists for more than 1,000 years.

Social scientists learn about human interactions by studying historical figures.

During the late 1800s, scientists began to use more experimental methods to develop theories for human behavior. In 1879, German physician Wilhelm Wundt opened the first psychology lab at the University of Leipzig in Germany. That event is often cited as marking the official beginning of psychology as a scientific field, and Wundt became the first person to call himself a psychologist.

The practice of lying on a couch (below) while talking to a psychologist began with Sigmund Freud (opposite).

In the early days of psychology, the focus was on **conscious** human thought and behavior. But in the early 1900s, Austrian physician Sigmund Freud developed the theory of personality, which looked at a patient's **unconscious** mind for insight into the way that person behaved. From his clinical work with hysteria patients, Freud hypothesized that the experiences of childhood shaped an adult's personality. He theorized their **neurosis** had its roots in a forgotten past traumatic experience. While undergoing Freud's treatment of psycho-analysis, a patient talked about his problems with an analyst and addressed unconscious thoughts from dreams and fantasies. The past trauma would be emotionally and intellectually confronted, and then, theoretically, the problem would disappear. In his book *The Psychopathology of Everyday Life*, Freud

gives examples of how a person's unconscious thinking reveals itself through dreams and unintentional speech (now known as "Freudian slips"). Freud believed people developed mental disorders when the conflicts in their unconscious became too much to handle. Although he wanted to help others with their mental issues, he had problems of his own, such as phobias (abnormal fears) about travel as well as a cigar addiction. Though controversial, his theories profoundly influenced the field of psychology and became the topics of art, films, and books.

CARL JUNG

Swiss psychiatrist Carl Jung (1875–1961) had a famous friendship with psychologist Sigmund Freud. Although they both agreed a person should analyze his or her fantasies and dreams, they disagreed on how to go about doing so. This led to an argument. Jung then discovered analytical psychology, a field that explores both a person's conscious and unconscious thinking. He used the terms introvert (shy) and extrovert (outgoing) to describe the two main attitudes people exhibit to the world. To better understand the mind, Jung also studied people who believed in the occult, or magical powers. After he spent 16 years writing what is known in English as *The Red Book*, the work was locked away in a Swiss bank vault until 48 years after his death. Unlike his other scientific publications, this book was about Jung analyzing his own dreams as well as fantasies in which he travels to the land of the dead.

While Freud was studying how unconscious thoughts influenced the way people acted, Russian physiologist Ivan Pavlov was developing a concept called behaviorism. Pavlov had invented a surgical procedure that allowed him to observe an animal's organs while the creature did most of its normal activities. Previously, scientists had used dissection to study organs and had to guess at how they functioned in real life.

In observing the behavior of dogs, Pavlov realized that people could be **conditioned** to act in certain ways, too. In his most famous experiment, Pavlov showed that dogs could be conditioned to salivate. Pavlov rang a bell (known as a neutral stimulus) each time he fed the dogs. Repeating this several times, Pavlov then decided to see what would happen if he rang the bell without any food present. The dogs salivated to the mere sound because they had learned to associate the bell with food. Pavlov's work became applicable to many circumstances, such as treating people with phobias. Because of the way Pavlov conducted his research, other scientists began to study animal and human behavior with similar objective methods.

Pavlov's conditioning experiments grew out of prior research on dogs' saliva and digestive systems.

Scientists were also studying people's behavior in government and society. British economist John Stuart Mill revolutionized the way people thought about their individual freedom within society, thanks to his 1859 book, *On Liberty*. He famously argued that the only circumstance in which society had the right to control individuals was "whenever, in short, there is a definite damage, or a definite risk of damage, either to an individual or to the public." Although influenced by his utilitarian upbringing (which taught him that actions are right if they're good for the majority of people), Mill still

DID YOU KNOW? Humans are said to be capable of having only 150 stable social relationships, known as Dunbar's Number (for anthropologist Robin Dunbar, pictured at left).

Above: Vladimir Lenin's social reforms also brought about an oppressive dictatorship.

defended the rights of the individual within the population. He was a staunch supporter of gender equality and women having the right to vote. Believing the community's majority often squelches an individual's liberties, Mill was an activist for political and social change.

Another social theorist was German economist and sociologist Karl Marx. In 1848, Marx published the **Communist** *Manifesto,* which argued that society had become a way of imprisoning people who were meant to be free. Western Europe was going through a time of revolutions, and Marx seized on the opportunity to make people question their societal values and motives. Marx's beliefs (known as Marxism) included the ideas that no one should own land or have rights to inheritances. Although critics pointed out philosophical flaws, the growing supporters of Marxism said that it gave hope of a better life to poor workers. The Russian Social Democratic Party was formed in 1898 to spread Marxism. Because the ideas were based on an industrial society and Russia was, for the most part, an agricultural one, Marxism did not take hold at first. It needed political theorist Vladimir Lenin to rally Russia's industrial workers and lead a revolution in 1917. Afterward, Marxist-Leninist political ideology governed Russia until December 25, 1991—the day Russia's Soviet Union announced the end of the world's first communist-led state.

On the other side of the world, German-American anthropologist Franz Boas (1858–1942) was discovering how people from different cultures lived. He began observing native peoples of the Pacific Northwest, such as the Inuit, in the 1880s. Boas criticized the popular view that Western culture was superior to other civilizations and argued that non-Western cultures weren't primitive or savage. "Civilization is not something absolute," he said. "Our ideas and conceptions are true only so far as our civilization goes." By this,

he meant that each society has its own interpretations of **ethical** standards and good manners. After moving to the United States in 1887, Boas worked for the Smithsonian Institution and then became Columbia University's first anthropology professor. As he was developing the theories behind anthropology, he worked to disprove the scientific racism of his day. In the 1930s, he spoke out against Germany's dictator Adolf Hitler and the dangers of believing in the Nazi ideology of a master race. The Nazis (and other groups that did not like Boas's conclusions that all cultures were equal) burned his 1911 book, *The Mind of Primitive Man*.

Remains have helped scientists reconstruct Pompeii's victims (opposite) and prehistoric humans (above).

Meanwhile, other anthropologists were studying the 780,000-year-old Peking Man, early prehistoric humans, and societies that practiced human sacrifice, such as the Aztecs of Mexico. Still other anthropologists were researching the Incas of Peru, who built a wall around their ancient capital with rocks fitted together so tightly that not even a hair could slide between them. Some anthropologists were studying excavations of ancient cities such as Pompeii, which had been buried in volcanic ash since A.D. 79. The ash preserved the city in the moment the disaster happened, with families still cowered together, criminals chained, and art intact, all providing information to social scientists about how a once-thriving Roman society had lived.

TRY IT OUT! Find out if weather affects mood: Create a survey asking the same 10 people on a sunny day and a rainy day to rate how they are feeling from 1 to 10. Ask questions about their happiness and level of energy. Analyze the results!

EXPERIMENTS AND REFORMS

DURING THE HOLOCAUST OF WORLD WAR II, APPROXimately 6 million Jews were killed in concentration camps and other facilities throughout Germany and its occupied territories. Such a systematic murdering required the cooperation of hundreds of thousands of citizens and military personnel. People—including social scientists—have often wondered how such atrocities could possibly occur. As often happens in science, the quest to discover one outcome can easily reveal another. In the case of the Stanford Prison Experiment, psychology researchers stumbled into unexpected territory. Their observations ultimately contributed to an ethical question: What makes good people do bad things?

In 1971, the U.S. Office of Naval Research funded an experiment on conflicts between military guards and prisoners. Led by Dr.

At least 1.1 million people died at Poland's Auschwitz concentration camp.

Philip Zimbardo of Stanford University, the two-week experiment intended to study how prisoners adapt when they are powerless. Zimbardo and his team chose 24 college males out of more than 70 applicants and assigned at random the roles of prisoners and guards.

A mock prison was set up in the basement of Stanford University's psychology building. On August 17, 1971, a police car picked up the volunteers in a mass arrest. After the prisoners' booking at the "prison," it didn't take long for the experiment to blur the lines between reality and make-believe. "The first day they came there, it was a little prison set up in a basement with fake cell doors," Zimbardo said later, "and by the second day, it was a real prison created in the minds of each prisoner, each guard, and also of the staff."

Guards were given uniforms and told they needed to make their captives feel powerless, doing whatever was necessary to keep order—short of physically harming anyone. Left to their own devices, the guards became increasingly aggressive and cruel. Prisoners were stripped, blindfolded, deprived of sleep, forced to do pushups as punishment, and addressed by only their identification numbers. Psychologists quickly realized the guards' actions were eerily similar to those of the Nazis who ran concentration camps.

By the second day, a prisoner rebellion had broken out. "Bad" prisoners were sent to solitary confinement—a closet known as "The Hole." Well-behaved prisoners were given a "privilege cell" with special food and enlisted as spies against their fellow inmates. The experimental prison had become real to everyone involved, including Zimbardo. One of his graduate students pointed out that he was no longer acting like a research psychologist. "I'm not the researcher at all," Zimbardo admitted. "Even my posture changes— when I walk through the prison yard, I'm walking with my hands behind my back, which I never in my life do, the way generals walk

From 1934 to 1963, prisoners attempted to escape 14 times from California's Alcatraz Federal Penitentiary.

MARY LEAKEY

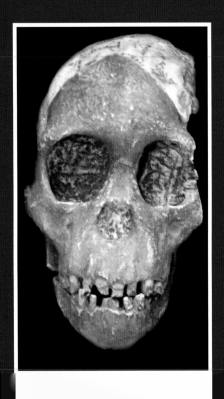

Born in London in 1913, Mary Leakey was a talented child artist. "I dug things up," she recalled later. "I was curious. And then I liked to draw what I found." In 1934, she illustrated archaeologist and anthropologist Dr. Louis Leakey's book *Adam's Ancestors*. After the two married in 1937, they moved to Africa, becoming one of history's most famous husband-and-wife scientific teams. While excavating Tanzania's Olduvai Gorge, Mary discovered a skull dating back more than 18 million years. It belonged to *Proconsul africanus*, an early ancestor to apes and humans that developed into two different species. In 1959, Mary discovered a 2-million-year-old, small-brained early human now called *Paranthropus boisei* (left). The next year, she and Louis found a human species, *Homo habilis*, that appeared to have used stone tools. The Leakeys also uncovered remains of extinct three-toed horses. Mary's 1978 discovery of early **hominid** footprints proved they walked on two feet. She continued her studies until her 1996 death in Kenya.

when they're inspecting troops." Prisoners soon began to show signs of **psychosis**. After just six days, the experiment was ended. The results of the study showed how prisons demoralize inmates, making them feel helpless and hopeless. But it also showed how people given authority can abuse power. Though the study's integrity had been compromised, it suggested that certain situations are capable of overriding someone's usual tendencies—and dictating behavior. However, other scientists have criticized this conclusion.

"Power tends to corrupt, and absolute power corrupts absolutely," said English politician Lord Acton, nearly a century before the Stanford Prison Experiment. Some political scientists believed a parliamentary government such as Lord Acton's—in which chosen ministers advise a chief of state with no clear separation of powers—would be better for the U.S. than the presidential system in place. Even 28th U.S. president Woodrow Wilson, who had a PhD in political science, agreed. Wilson felt the U.S. Constitution was outdated and too easily corrupted—and that the separate governmental branches meant to provide "checks and balances" actually made it impossible to tell who was responsible. In such books as *Congressional Government*, Wilson

The U.S. Capitol houses the federal legislative chambers of the Senate and House of Representatives.

advocated for a government that relieved the burdens of its citizens through programs that bordered on socialism—a theory based upon industries being controlled by the government instead of private individuals. While Wilson was president, the U.S. government took more control over American industries, issuing tariff, business, and banking reforms. The government lowered import and export taxes, established the Federal Trade Commission (FTC) to investigate illegal businesses, and helped farmers get loans.

DID YOU KNOW? In ancient times, people traded items such as salt, livestock, shark teeth (left), and precious stones rather than money.

Above: Mother Teresa expressed "love of humanity" in her service to others.

As political scientists, Wilson and others utilized different methods to measure and collect data for studying government and politics. Some social scientists base their measurements on what is known as rational choice theory. This is the idea that most people are motivated by making money and that they calculate costs versus the possibilities of profit before taking action. Since they cannot have everything they want, people calculate and choose the action that will bring them the best result. This leads them to prioritize their choices. Over the centuries, rational choice theorists have come to rely more heavily on math to compile their data, calculating the money spent on producing and distributing products. Critics of the rational choice theory argue that if individuals base their actions only on what they can gain monetarily, then the theory is incomplete, because it does not account for selfless acts.

Social scientists have long tried to understand the cause and motivation behind philanthropy (the behavior to improve the welfare of others, such as donating money to a charity). Sociologists such as Dr. Rene Bekkers from the University of Amsterdam are fascinated by who gives, what amount they give, and why. To gather measureable data, Bekkers and other social scientists use social psychological scales. In these scales, philanthropists rate how much they agree with statements such as "It is hard for me to support causes I do not benefit from" or "We have to make this world a better place for the next generation."

Sociologists collect and measure data from the different social science branches to formulate a theory on human philanthropy. Some sociologists believe giving might aid in survival, as witnessed by Dr. Frans de Waal's animal behavior studies of chimpanzees. In his 1996 book, *Good Natured: The Origins of Right and Wrong in Humans and Other Animals,* he describes how chimpanzees give and

reciprocate—and the consequences they face when they act selfishly. When members of a chimpanzee troop refuse to share their food and groom each other, they are driven away, which will hurt their chances for survival. In this case, a failure to reciprocate is met with a serious consequence. When people need help and cannot reciprocate, the generosity of those who are able becomes a powerful act. It corrects an imbalance in social relationships within a society.

Billionaire philanthropist Warren Buffett, who holds a master's degree in economics, has taken a pledge with billionaire Bill Gates to eventually give away more than half his fortune. At a banquet to encourage other billionaires to take the "Giving Pledge," Buffett said, "If you have trouble living on $500 million, I'm gonna put out a book, *How to Live on $500 Million*. Think about whether the other $500 million might do more for humanity than it will for you and your family." Social scientists have discovered that both reciprocal giving and giving "something for nothing" are ways of being good members of one's own species. Giving increases both the giver's and the receiver's survival chances, as well as that of the society as a whole.

Warren Buffett (left) has donated billions to the foundation run by Bill (right) and Melinda Gates.

TRY IT OUT! Should you invest? Imagine if you put $1 into an account that earns interest at a 50 percent rate. By the third day, you will earn interest on top of your interest. At the end of seven days, your $1 will grow to $11.39 because of **compound interest**!

JEKYLL AND HYDE

A SOCIETY CLASSIFIES ITS "GOOD CITIZENS" AS THOSE who follow the rules. These rules are referred to as social norms. Different cultures have their own social norms, and what is considered offensive behavior in one part of the world may be perfectly acceptable in another. An example of this exists in parts of the Middle East, India, and Africa, where people eat their food with only their right hand. It is considered bad manners to use the left hand for eating or shaking hands. Each society has methods for enforcing its rules. In some countries, for instance, a person found guilty of stealing may be imprisoned, while in other parts of the world, he may have his hand cut off.

Social scientists study social norms, examining how they became part of the society and if the rules have changed over time. There are specialties in psychology and sociology that focus on the study of deviant behavior.

The tea ceremony of the Berber people represents a cultural norm of North Africa.

This is the behavior of individuals and groups who break social norms.

Scientists judge this sort of behavior by when and where it occurred. For example, although murder is considered a crime in most places, it is often permitted in times of war or self-defense. Likewise, fighting is not allowed in school or church. However, boxing and mixed martial arts (MMA) are considered sporting events and are widely watched for entertainment.

Robert Louis Stevenson's 1886 novella, *The Strange Case of Dr. Jekyll and Mr. Hyde*, is about a man who has traits, or characteristics, known in psychology as dissociative identity disorder (DID). Once called multiple personality disorder, DID is a mental condition in which the afflicted person has two or more identities controlling his or her behavior. When one personality takes over, the person suffering from DID has no memory of the other identity. In Stevenson's story, Dr. Jekyll and Mr. Hyde are the same man: the upstanding Dr. Henry Jekyll and the evil Edward Hyde personality.

Today, Maryland's Towson University professor Dr. Bethany Brand researches DID and treats patients suffering from the disorder. People who have DID often experienced abuse or another long-term trauma throughout their childhood. Rather than developing a single sense of self, their minds form different identities. According to Brand, DID patients "space out and lose track of minutes or hours" and even hurt themselves without recalling how they did it.

Researchers believe DID may afflict 1 percent or more of the population. It is about as common as other mental conditions such as bipolar disorder and schizophrenia. Brand remarks that DID "is much more subtle than any Hollywood portrayal." Making treatment more complex, DID patients often have other disorders as well, such as depression, drug abuse, and post-traumatic stress disorder.

Psychologists such as Brand try to get all their clients' personality

A dream prompted author Robert Louis Stevenson (above) to draft his Jekyll-and-Hyde story (opposite).

ADAM SMITH

Adam Smith was born in 1723 in Scotland. When he was 14, he became a philosophy student at the University of Glasgow and, later, a member of the faculty. Smith was passionate about liberty and free speech during a period known as the Scottish Enlightenment. His book *The Wealth of Nations* was published in 1776 and is considered the first work of political economics. In it, Smith states that a nation's success is measured by what is known today as gross national product (GNP) rather than the amount of gold and silver it has. He explains that when people act upon their self-interests, it improves society. These ideas became the basis for **capitalism**. Smith had most of his other works destroyed as he neared death. In secret, he gave away much of his money to charities. On July 17, 1790, he died at the age of 67.

states working together. Since patients often switch personalities when they think of bad memories, get angry, or become frightened, psychologists gradually teach them to manage their thoughts and feelings. Brand also uses techniques such as hypnosis to help her DID patients who have trouble sleeping. "I want you to breathe slowly and deeply and imagine being in a safe place," she tells them. Eventually, the patient can sleep more restfully and handle stress without switching personalities.

Anthropologists often become well known in their fields by traveling to dangerous places to discover new things. Dr. Napoleon Chagnon has been featured in the *New York Times* as one of the most famous and controversial anthropologists in recent times. While researching the Amazon jungle's Yanomami tribe, Chagnon survived encounters with both a jaguar and a 15-foot (4.6 m) anaconda that lunged at him while he tried to drink from a stream. The very people he was researching once even tried to kill him in his sleep. "Indiana Jones had nothing on me," Chagnon said.

Yanomami women often prepare meals with tapioca, the starch of the South American cassava plant.

Growing up among 11 siblings in a poor Michigan family, Chagnon learned how to be independent and use a shotgun at an early age. He made use of both those skills in his fieldwork. In 1964, he began conducting anthropology research near the Venezuela-Brazil border. In his best-selling book *Yanomamö: The Fierce People*, Chagnon described his first encounter with the tribesmen: "Immense wads of green tobacco were stuck between their lower teeth and lips making them look even more hideous, and strands of dark-green slime dripped or hung from their noses." This slime was the hallucinogenic drug ebene.

DID YOU KNOW? In 2010, a Harvard study reported that participants' minds wandered an average of 46.9 percent of the time during everyday activities such as eating or watching TV.

Above: Many Yanomami women decorate their faces with paint and piercings.

Chagnon wanted to study the genealogy (family history) and warfare of the tribe. His anthropological training had taught him that fights usually break out among groups over food and resources such as gold or land. However, during his first 17 months with the Yanomami, he observed the tribesmen fighting over women instead.

The Yanomami soon nicknamed Chagnon "Shaki," which means "pesky bee." But Chagnon continued working with the tribe into the 1990s. By his last trip to the jungle in 1995, he had collected information on approximately 4,000 Yanomami, tracing some families as far back as the 1800s. The patterns he analyzed based on this data made him a pioneer in the fields of sociobiology and human behavioral ecology. Through his work, Chagnon also helped vaccinate 1,000 Yanomami against measles. When he was elected into the prestigious National Academy of Sciences, Chagnon and others viewed it as vindication, because some journalists and anthropologists had criticized both his methods and motivations. Those who took a more charitable view applauded Chagnon for daring to suggest that humans have a greater tendency toward aggressive rather than peaceful behavior. Based on his studies, Chagnon wrote, "Violence ... may be the principal driving force behind the evolution of culture."

Many social scientists focus on the study of violence, especially the expense, effects, and changing state of warfare around the world. Some of humankind's groundbreaking scientific and technological advancements, such as radar and the Internet, came about because of war or the threat of war. However, many innovations that have improved societies developed without dangerous conflicts. War has costly economic consequences, with buildings and structures destroyed, massive public debt, and, of course, loss of human life. From bone studies, anthropologists know 20 percent of people died

violent deaths during the Stone Age, whereas less than 1 percent suffer the same fate today.

Political scientists such as Yale University's Dr. Paul Bracken have been studying how countries are using modern financial warfare. In 2007, Bracken wrote in a Foreign Policy Research Institute article, "The U.S. is increasingly using financial warfare to punish international actors, blocking the overseas bank accounts of North Korean, Iranian, and Russian companies involved in illicit activities such as nuclear and conventional weapons proliferation." Economic warfare may block resources such as fuel, but financial warfare hurts where it counts most—money in an account just disappears. Bracken states, "In many respects, conventional economic warfare is like carpet bombing; financial warfare is like precision strike." The ability to attack and defend a country's financial institutions has huge economic and political consequences. Because of this, social scientists think that financial and economic warfare will increasingly become the weapons of choice.

Navy SEALs (opposite) and other U.S. special forces engaged in actual warfare after the September 11 attacks (below).

TRY IT OUT! Find out if clothing color influences first impressions. Have volunteers wearing different-colored shirts say the same sentence to a group. Ask the group to rate on a scale of 1 to 10 how smart, fun, and kind the person is!

FUTURE OF HUMANKIND

THE SOCIAL SCIENCES OFTEN TRY TO IMPROVE THE world we live in. Some social scientists conduct research on how to reduce crime, help the homeless, ease intolerance, and earn more money. With modern technology, it is now possible for different countries to share information, make comparisons, and even conduct surveys that aid in furthering scientific research.

As new technology emerges, social scientists are encountering ethical dilemmas. Doctors can take **deoxyribonucleic acid (DNA)** from three different parents to prevent disease in an embryo. Some believe our brains will one day be capable of uploading to a computer, allowing great-great-grandchildren to converse with us. In 2013, scientists at MIT were able to implant memories into mice brains—a technology that could help Alzheimer's patients who suffer from memory loss. But each of these types of research has critics who warn that it is morally questionable.

Today's social scientists study how both genetics and environment affect behavior.

In his book *In 100 Years*, Ignacio

Palacios-Huerta, an economist from the London School of Economics, reports that the next century could see the average human life span reach 100 years. Medical advances could help people manipulate **genes**, improving memory and intelligence. With people living longer, Palacios-Huerta says, careers would change. People could work hard for 30 years and then spend many years performing lower-effort work. Robots will likely automate more jobs. People will be more educated, leading to a society that calls for democracy and peace. Video conferences might be replaced by holograms. Climate change may make more people want to move to Siberia and Canada. Since people will make more money, the world's poor could live like today's middle class.

Economic research helps plan for overall future food needs (opposite) and individuals' aging processes (below).

Economics researcher Meredith Whitney predicts American production for fuel, cars, and clothing will increase in the next few years. That is because the price to manufacture goods in China is not as low as it once was, by the time overseas shipping amounts are added into the equation. She also thinks businesses and people will move more into America's middle states in the next 30 years because of the lower taxes and abundant resources. According to the U.S. Department of Agriculture, such resources as grain will be in high demand globally by 2021, and the exports of U.S. crops could increase by 28 percent.

The study of anthropology is helpful to those whose future work requires relating to and communicating with the public. Anthropologists tackle biological and cultural problems, such as whether African American medical patients are more likely to suffer from high blood pressure because of genetics or diet. Future business professionals, through anthropology studies, can learn how other societies make and spend money to find opportunities in the global marketplace. Anthropologists are still trying to understand

ÉMILE DURKHEIM

Émile Durkheim (1858–1917) came from a long line of Jewish rabbis. Growing up in France, Durkheim first attended a Jewish school but decided to switch to a non-religious institution. After completing his studies at École Normale Supérieure, he became a teacher. The young Durkheim brought the study of social science into the curriculum of all French schools. Every Saturday, he taught a public social science course, which included topics such as suicide, crime, religion, law, and family. In the 1890s, he published several works, including *The Rules of Sociological Method*, and founded the first journal for the social sciences in France. Durkheim's theories—such as how societies transform from simple to complex—and terms he coined—such as "collective consciousness"—went on to influence the work of other sociologists, including his nephew, Marcel Mauss. Above all, Durkheim wanted to establish sociology as an independent branch of science—a goal he achieved.

both the past and present variations in humans and what the social and cultural times were like. In the future, anthropologists and archaeologists might study objects such as the iPod to try to understand what people were like in the early 2000s.

Dr. Jim Dator is a political science professor at the University of Hawaii and conducts research in futures studies. This new social science field delves into possible alternative futures to give humans more control over what might be coming. According to Dator, "Any useful statement about the future should appear to be ridiculous." When asked to comment on the futures of work, Dator has said, "The way we live now will seem unbelievable 50, 100, 1,000 years from now. The most ordinary things about our daily lives will seem strange and exotic." To make educated predictions about the future, Dator also studies the past. "The number of humans began to grow because the evolution of speech enabled us to orga- nize ourselves much better than ever before." Because of a grow- ing human population, local food sources were diminished. People either died or developed new technologies to grow and trap food, leading eventually to cities and the invention of work. Dator offers four alternative futures for what work might be like: we will have continued global growth; we will experience an economic/environ- mental collapse; we will become more disciplined to meet industrial and information needs; or we will become hunters and gatherers again to survive.

Some psychologists are focusing their research on the very people who will grow up to shape the future: middle-schoolers and teenagers. Scientists want to know what drives some youth to abuse drugs, get in trouble with police, bully, and harm themselves. "More

Social scientists are already studying how Apple's iPod, released in 2001, has helped shape modern culture.

DID YOU KNOW? The underground Terracotta Army (above) was carved by 700,000 forced laborers to protect the tomb of Chinese emperor Qin Shi Huang.

young people under age 35 die of accidents, suicides, homicides, and the effects of smoking, drinking, and drugs than from all the major diseases in the world," said psychologist Dr. Lewis P. Lipsitt. "And all of these things are preventable."

Mentors and parents have significant influence over a teenager's behavior. However, some behavior is biological. Hormones help teens grow into adults, but the increased biological surges can make even the most nicely mannered young person act out. As a teen's brain develops, it is very susceptible to addictions such as alcohol and tobacco. Magnetic resonance imaging (MRI)—magnets and radio waves that take internal body pictures—from brain studies have shown the brain (including the part that helps make decisions) does not fully develop until around age 25. This helps explain why teens are associated with more risk-taking behavior. Teens tend to choose riskier actions when they drive with peers in the car compared with driving alone. Because of this, some states have raised the driving age and limited how many passengers a teen can have in the car.

Social scientists are also studying the long-term effects of bullying. Dr. Susan Limber, a psychologist at Clemson University, has found that 20 percent of middle-school kids in the U.S. admit to bullying others. Youngsters who bully are more likely to get into fights, steal, smoke, drink, have weapons, and quit school than non-bullying kids. The negative impact doesn't stop there. By age 24, nearly 60 percent of boys who bullied others in middle school have at least 1 criminal conviction.

Contrary to popular belief, recent research has found that bullies aren't usually loners. In fact, they are quite often popular. Continuing to act as though bullying is caused by low self-esteem "may produce more confident bullies," Limber said. When kids, parents, and teachers intervene and establish acceptable behaviors in the school

through bully prevention programs, it lowers the instances of this tormenting behavior.

Some social scientists are researching how young people and adults can harness their emotions in positive ways through emotional intelligence (EI). Psychologists say that if people could learn to identify, use, understand, and manage their emotions, they could solve problems—and be more successful. "Teaching emotional intelligence can help children find occupations that are most suited to their interest and abilities, have satisfying relationships with others, and become active and productive members of their communities," says Dr. Cary Cherniss. As the former spiritual leader of India Mahatma Gandhi once said, "If we are to teach real peace in this world, and if we are to carry on a real war against war, we shall have to begin with the children."

The social and behavioral sciences are useful in understanding topics such as cultural, political, and behavioral patterns, whether those behaviors are displayed in classrooms, jungles, or prisons. By studying the accomplishments and failures of humans throughout history, social scientists have continued to ask questions about behavior and relationships in society. Social scientists' theories lead to informed guesses about the future. Their methods of scientific research may be some of the best tools we possess to improve the world around us.

Future leaders (opposite) can study the success of Gandhi's (below) emotionally intelligent style.

TRY IT OUT! Test if someone has a photographic memory: Show the tester a card with a random sequence of 9 numbers for 30 seconds. Remove the card and ask him or her to say the alphabet before writing down the numbers from memory!

capitalism: an economic and political system in which a country's trade and industry are controlled by private owners (rather than the state) for profit

communist: having to do with the political and economic system in which all goods and property are owned by the state and shared by all members of the public

compound interest: additional money paid on both the original sum of money and all the money it has earned

conditioned: having one's behavior modified through negative and positive reinforcement

conscious: having knowledge and awareness of one's surroundings

cultures: particular groups in a society that share behaviors and characteristics that are accepted as normal by that group

deoxyribonucleic acid (DNA): a substance found in every living thing that determines the species and individual characteristics of that thing

ethical: related to conduct of right and wrong behavior

genes: hereditary units that transfer traits from a parent to a child

hominid: a primate of a family that includes humans and their ancient ancestors

hypothesize: to make an educated guess; to suggest an explanation based on a limited amount of evidence

neurosis: a mild mental disorder (such as anxiety or depression) in which the person still has a sense of reality

psychosis: a mental disorder in which the person loses touch with reality

scientific method: a step-by-step method of research that includes making observations, forming hypotheses, performing experiments, and analyzing results

unconscious: related to the part of the mind that affects behavior and emotions

Backhouse, Roger E. *The Ordinary Business of Life: A History of Economics from the Ancient World to the Twenty-first Century*. Princeton, N.J.: Princeton University Press, 2002.

Bernard, H. Russell. *Research Methods in Anthropology: Qualitative and Quantitative Methods*. Walnut Creek, Calif.: AltaMira, 2002.

Ember, Carol R., Melvin Ember, and Peter N. Peregrine. *Anthropology*. 10th ed. Upper Saddle River, N.J.: Prentice Hall, 2002.

Johnson, Janet Buttolph, Richard A. Joslyn, and H. T. Reynolds. *Political Science Research Methods*. 4th ed. Washington, D.C.: CQ, 2001.

Kahn, Michael. *Basic Freud: Psychoanalytic Thought for the Twenty-first Century*. New York: Basic Books, 2002.

Meyerson, Daniel. *In the Valley of the Kings: Howard Carter and the Mystery of King Tutankhamun's Tomb*. New York: Ballantine Books, 2009.

Pickren, Wade E. *The Psychology Book*. New York: Sterling, 2014.

Zimbardo, Philip G. *The Lucifer Effect: Understanding How Good People Turn Evil*. New York: Random House, 2007.

NATIONAL GEOGRAPHIC EDUCATION: ANTHROPOLOGY
http://education.nationalgeographic.com/education/encyclopedia/anthropology/
This website contains more information about anthropology and its many fields.

NATIONAL GEOGRAPHIC KIDS: TUTANKHAMUN FACTS
http://www.ngkids.co.uk/did-you-know/Tutankhamun-facts
Learn about archaeologist Howard Carter's discovery of one of the most famous Egyptian pharaohs.

Note: Every effort has been made to ensure that the websites listed above are suitable for children, that they have educational value, and that they contain no inappropriate material. However, because of the nature of the Internet, it is impossible to guarantee that these sites will remain active indefinitely or that their contents will not be altered.